W9-CKI-177

Richardson I.S.D.
Wallace Elementary
9921 Kirkhaven Dr.
Dallas, TX 75238

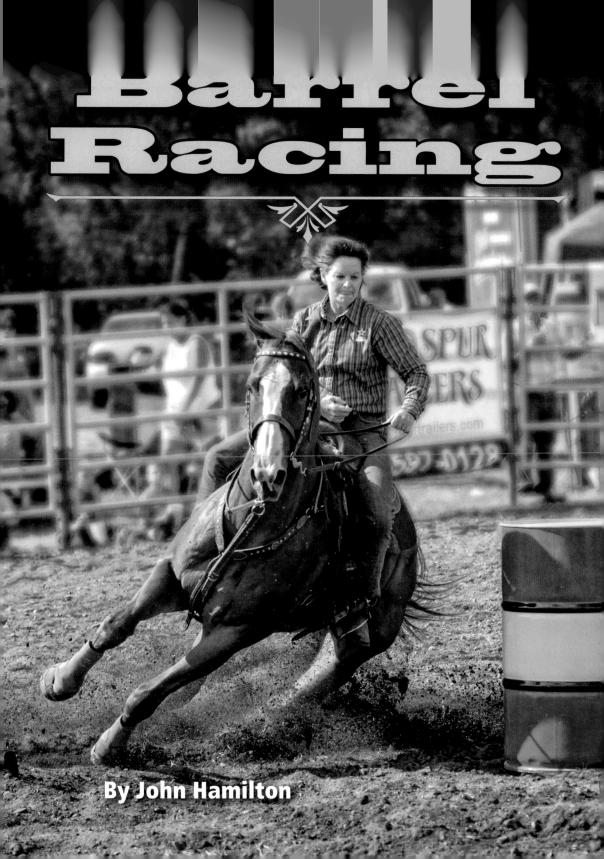

Barrel Racing

By John Hamilton

Visit us at
www.abdopublishing.com

Published by ABDO Publishing Company, PO Box 398166, Minneapolis, MN 55439. Copyright ©2014 by Abdo Consulting Group, Inc. International copyrights reserved in all countries. No part of this book may be reproduced in any form without written permission from the publisher. A&D Xtreme™ is a trademark and logo of ABDO Publishing Company.

Printed in the United States of America, North Mankato, Minnesota.
052013
012014

 PRINTED ON RECYCLED PAPER

Editor: Sue Hamilton
Graphic Design: John Hamilton
Cover: John Hamilton
Photos: All photos by John Hamilton, except: Tom Baker-pg 32; Getty Images-p. 9; Library of Congress-pg 8.

ABDO Booklinks
Web sites about rodeos are featured on our Book Links pages. These links are routinely monitored and updated to provide the most current information available. Web site: www.abdopublishing.com

Library of Congress Control Number: 2013931677

Cataloging-in-Publication Data

Hamilton, John.
 Barrel racing / John Hamilton.
   p. cm. -- (Xtreme rodeo)
ISBN 978-1-61783-978-8
1. Barrel racing--Juvenile literature.   I. Title.
791.8/4--dc23
                         2013931677

Contents

Barrel Racing

Many rodeo fans say barrel racing is their favorite event. It's no wonder why. Skilled cowgirls and their powerful horses tear around a cloverleaf pattern in a race against the clock. The sound of thundering hooves fills the air. Barrel racing is a thrilling event that pushes a cheering crowd to its feet.

At the last dash to the finish line, horses gallop more than 30 miles per hour (48 kph).

History

Early rodeos featured many women competitors. However, by the 1930s, opportunities for women grew scarce. Barrel racing may have been started by the wives and girlfriends of male rodeo competitors. Perhaps they got together for a friendly contest. Or they wanted to

display their own equestrian skills. At first, barrel racing was a sideshow to male-dominated rodeos. Today, it is a serious sport and very popular among rodeo fans.

"Rodeo" is a Spanish word used by early cowboys when they gathered up their cattle. The English translation is "round up."

Groups

In 1948, a group of women from Texas formed the Girls' Rodeo Association. They wanted more opportunities for women in professional rodeos. In 1981,  the association changed its name to the Women's Professional Rodeo Association (WPRA). Another  group that organizes the sport is the National Barrel Horse Association (NBHA).

Today, the WPRA, NBHA, and other groups bring the sport of barrel racing to hundreds of professional rodeos across the United States and Canada.

The Pattern

Competitors race around three barrels arranged in a cloverleaf pattern on the rodeo arena. The barrels are standard 55-gallon (208-liter) metal or plastic drums. They are placed to form a triangle. The first two barrels, one right and one left, are at the front of the arena where the rider enters. A third barrel is placed in back.

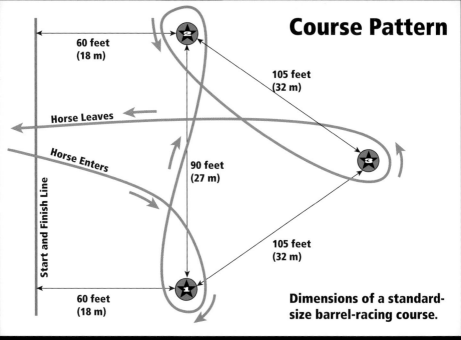

Course Pattern

60 feet
(18 m)

105 feet
(32 m)

Horse Leaves

Horse Enters

90 feet
(27 m)

Start and Finish Line

105 feet
(32 m)

60 feet
(18 m)

Dimensions of a standard-size barrel-racing course.

The Race

Barrel racing is a timed event. Competitors race against the clock and each other. The horse and rider enter the arena at a full gallop. Speed and agility will determine the winner. Riders train their horses to turn as close to a barrel as possible without knocking it over and causing a penalty.

In most professional rodeos, a beam projected by an electronic timer marks both the start and finish line. When the beam is first crossed, the timer begins. Time is measured in hundredths of a second. The first barrel is called the "money barrel." A rider's final time often depends on how well the horse maneuvers around this crucial part of the course.

An electronic timer is used to record a barrel racer's score.

After crossing the starting line, riders can choose the right or left barrel first. Horses favor one side or the other, much like humans are either right- or left-handed. A right turn around the right barrel would then be followed by left turns around the last two barrels. A left turn around the left barrel would be followed by right turns around the last two barrels. Either path forms a cloverleaf pattern.

If a rider knocks over a barrel, a five-second penalty is added to the score. Competitors who run past a barrel and off the cloverleaf pattern are disqualified.

After maneuvering around the third barrel, the horse and rider make a dash for the finish line. A winning time in a small arena might range from 13 to 14 seconds. In a larger arena, a winning run might take 17 to 18 seconds.

Riders

Barrel racing is considered a women's rodeo event, although some men do occasionally compete. Mostly, however, it's the cowgirls's chance to show off their skills. Barrel racing requires great horsemanship. Riders learn to control their horses with rein handling, sitting in different saddle positions, and "talking" to their horses during a ride. Winning riders and horses work as a team.

Young barrel racers can compete in youth and novice divisions.

Horses

American quarter horses often make great barrel racers. They are good at sprinting short distances, can take tight turns, and learn directions quickly. Other breeds, such as Appaloosas and Morgans, are also used in the sport. The most important factors are a horse's speed, acceleration, and ability to work well with a human partner. A champion barrel-racing horse can cost more than $100,000.

Equipment

Barrel racers use Western saddles that are slightly smaller and lighter than standard roping saddles. A good saddle can cost $1,200 or more. The type of bridle used depends on the horse and how much control is needed. Bell boots and wraparound splints help protect a horse's hooves and legs during competition.

Professional barrel racers wear long-sleeved shirts, boots, and a Western-style hat. Safety helmets and shin guards are also sometimes worn. If a rider uses spurs, the rowels are always blunted and turn freely. Some riders use a quirt, a short-handled riding whip. Quirts are not used to punish. Riders communicate with their horses by thumping them on their flank. Many riders use voice commands, which make quirts unnecessary.

The Professional Rodeo Cowboys Association (PRCA) has strict rules to make sure rodeo livestock are treated humanely. Veterinarians are always on hand at PRCA-sanctioned rodeos to care for the animals.

Glossary

American Quarter Horse

A breed of horse that is famous for its speed, agility, and fast acceleration. It is called a quarter horse because it is often faster than any other horse over short distances, such as a quarter-mile (.4-km) sprint. Many barrel-racing horses are American quarter horses.

Equestrian

Something that relates to horse riding.

Professional Rodeo Cowboys Association

The PRCA is the largest and oldest rodeo sanctioning organization in the world. It ensures that rodeos meet high standards in working conditions and livestock welfare. Located in Colorado Springs, Colorado, it sanctions about 600 rodeos in the United States and Canada.

Quirt

A type of riding whip with two ends, called falls. Quirts are often made of leather. They are used to guide a horse.

Rein

A long strap attached to a horse's bit or noseband, used to guide or slow the animal. Reins are usually made of leather or nylon. Many barrel racers use a single closed rein that is easier to retrieve if dropped.

Timed Event

A rodeo event, such as barrel racing, in which contestants compete against the clock and themselves. The other kind of rodeo contest is the rough stock event, such as bull riding, which pits human

Index